THE YES / NO
TAROT ORACLE

Also by Eleanor Piper

TAROT BOOKS
THE LOVERS' SPREAD: A Tarot Guide to
Relationship Compatibility

NOVELS
The Grim – a novella

SHORT STORY COLLECTIONS
Between Stops

THE YES / NO TAROT ORACLE

with
a keyword guide to the cards' meanings
& an aide-mémoire for the Minor Arcana

Eleanor Piper

THE YES / NO
TAROT ORACLE

Originally published by Authors' Online 2012
Reissued, with permission, by MerrieOak Publishing 2015

Copyright © Eleanor Piper 2009
Diagrams © Siobhan Smith 2009
Cover art and illustrations © Jo Spaul 2009
Cover design © Jamie Day 2009

A CIP catalogue record for this book
is available from the British Library

ISBN 978 0 9931600 2 8

MerrieOak Publishing
England

This book is also available in e-book format
ISBN 978 0 9931982 2 9

The future is not predetermined.

You have free will and the responsibility to exercise it.

Table of contents

Table of contents (continued)

Table of contents (continued)

Table of contents (continued)

Introduction

THE PURPOSE OF THIS BOOK
This book is designed for two purposes:

- firstly as a yes / no oracle

- secondly as a key word guide to the meanings of the cards

Over the years I have found that there was very little information readily available on interpreting yes or no answers from the cards. This is gradually changing as people begin to write about how they find answers to questions that ask for a simple yes or no answer.

In this book I have set out the positive and negative interpretations for each card, and as such I hope that this book will help those of you who want a simple yes / no oracular guide.

HANDLE WITH CARE
Some things to be aware of:

One of the reasons the yes / no answer information has been kept to a minimum by Tarot practitioners in the past is, I feel, mainly due to the worry that people who have not worked with the cards for any length of time will be unaware of just how slippery the cards can be in their responses to a question. Newer readers may also be unaware of how readily the cards respond to strong emotion: giving the desired answer – which is easiest to find in the ether, as the questioner unwittingly projects it – rather than the oracular answer which lies a little further into the veil.

Developing one's intuition, learning to discern it from the voices of ego, keeping it free from the persuasions of others, and learning to *actually* listen to it, is something which in my experience can only be grasped over time through trial and error. ~ I've been working on this skill for decades, and even now I find times when my brain shouts down, or pooh-poohs, what my intuition tells me … and I suffer for it every time. Consider yourself warned.

– In short, quick yes / no answers need to be handled with extreme care.

If you have any doubts about taking a yes / no reading, I would recommend a multi-card layout rather than a single card spread (see below). Or alternatively you can consult an experienced Tarot Reader.

METHODS OF READING A YES / NO ORACLE
The Yes / No Tarot Oracle can either be used to provide a quick, one card: yes or no answer, or can be used in association with the key word guide as part of a more in depth multi-card reading. Please see **Using This Book** for more information on these two types of reading.

MEMORIZING THE CARDS

The other purpose of this book is to help new readers remember the meanings of each card: as such I have included a Key Word Guide for each card.

These guides mostly use short, descriptive sentences and key words which should help you to memorize how each of the cards can be interpreted in a reading.

The Key Word Guides can also act as a quick reference point for those times when you urgently need a prompt for the upright or reversed meanings associated with a particular card. ~ Please note, the YES / NO ORACLE only applies to a question that requires a yes / no answer. If you are conducting a more general reading and using this book to prompt your memory for the various meanings of the card you can ignore the positive or negative nature suggested by the yes / no oracle as it will not apply, instead go with the emphasis that your intuition (rather than this book) provides.

An aide-mémoire for the Minor Arcana is also included in the hope that this will help new-comers to the Tarot memorize the general meanings for each set of numbers or court cards in the Minor Arcana.

This is something that I would have loved to have had when I started learning about the Tarot cards, but could not find anywhere – which is why I have included it in this book. ... At some point in their career every Tarot reader may have a blank moment where the meaning of a card eludes them, it is hoped that by memorizing the aide-mémoire and using those general meanings in combination with the images on the card in question, the Tarot reader will be able to grasp the proper meaning, which in turn will prompt their intuition to pull in the answer to the question that was asked.

I trust that those of you who have recently begun to work with the Tarot will find this book particularly useful for solidifying the various meanings of each of the cards in your mind, both upright and reversed.

IMPRINTING THE CARDS

A couple of cautionary notes to new readers: firstly, as mentioned earlier, the cards respond to strong emotion and can give the answer that the person you are reading for projects on to them rather than giving the answer to the question that the person verbally asked. For example if someone asks, "Does he love me?" and they are emotionally screaming "He must love me!" the cards may well respond with *he loves you* rather than answering the actual question.

One way to help prevent this imprinting on the cards, is to centre yourself then ask the question again yourself on behalf of the person you are reading for while you shuffle the cards.

Personally I find I get a more accurate reading if I keep the other person's contact with the cards absolutely minimal – I may allow them to cut the deck once or twice after I have shuffled the cards, but that's it. However it is fine to use whichever method suits you best.

Each reader will develop their own preferred

method for preparing the cards for a reading, and should allow the person being read for to have as much or as little contact with the cards as the reader feels works best.

ASKING QUESTIONS
A second note of caution about reading an Oracle for someone: make sure the question they ask verbally is the question they actually mean to ask.

If the person you are reading for has a set goal in mind and is trying to gain insight into an important life choice, they will probably have thought through their question carefully. So you can be fairly sure they'll mean what they ask, and they probably require an in depth answer rather than a single card reading.

However people who ask questions on whim or without any real depth of thought, have a tendency to ask questions such as "Will I be rich?" or "Will I leave my husband?" Questions like these should really be being answered by the person asking them, for example if someone is asking "Will I leave my husband?" the unspoken answer is plainly "You've already made up your mind that this is a likely potential future, so why are you wasting both our time by even asking the question?" (Harsh? Definitely. That's why it remains an unspoken answer.*[see page.7]) **and there is the key: you will need to ask more questions in order to find out the true motive behind the question, and what has prompted it, in order to ferret out <u>the real question</u>**.

For example when someone asks "Will I be rich?"

there is a good chance that what they are really asking is "Will I be content?" or "Will I be happy?" Or perhaps they have a wealthy relative who is on his or her deathbed and they want to know if they are going to inherit? Even if they have just bought a lottery ticket, the real underlying question might still not be the one they present to you.

Without discovering the real question behind the question they've asked it is easy for the cards to provide a slippery and misleading Oracle....

Question: "Will I be rich?"

Answer: ***Judgement***, *YES – your motives and handling of a situation will have a direct bearing on its outcome.*

This is on the surface a perfectly fine reply, but the cards were actually answering the real underlying question the person had which was "Will I be content?", so the oracle is actually saying *if you live your life in a way that makes you content you will be content, and there is a good chance that this will happen; however, if you don't you won't.*

So the question will I be rich, gets the answer yes, but then the person never has two pennies to rub together and spends their life resenting the world for not handing everything to them on a platter and generally has a miserable time, and incidentally decides that the Tarot is a bunch of hooey.

And if the cards had actually answered the surface question in the example above, then the important part is the qualifying text, which I interpret to mean *the amount of effort you put in is the amount of reward you'll get out i.e.* Question: Will I be rich? Answer: YES, but only if you put in the necessary effort to become rich. … Also, note the lack of time scale.

* Unspoken answers… It is important to ascertain the level of vulnerability of the person who comes to you for a reading, and their motives behind asking each of their questions.

I know of a case where a young lady asked a rather cavalier reader whether her current beau was her Soul Mate. She believed she had found true love, that she had met the other half of her true self, and felt that he completed her totally.

The reader responded in the negative, and the young lady spent the rest of the afternoon in tears, and his answer probably haunted her throughout her relationship.

Now whether the young man was her Soul Mate or not, the reader should have found a more careful way to express the answer the cards were giving. I am not suggesting he should have lied, but he should have found a way to explain the answer in a way that didn't have her running off in tears and also possibly destroying her perfectly happy and (currently) successful relationship as an indirect result.

SACRED DUTY
Have a care when you provide an Oracle, it is a sacred duty, and people will tend to accord your words a lot of weight.

Make sure they understand that the cards only provide details on the most likely potential situation.

There are many outcomes to any situation and we all have *choice* as to how we approach events, people and the universe in general.

You should also remember that the cards may just be picking up on the answer that is closest, and being projected most strongly, into the ethers around them.

The future is never fixed.
People are fragile emotional creatures.

Keep those things in mind when you give an Oracle, make sure they are asking the real question, and you should be able to find the best way forwards during a reading. Good luck!

*

I hope you will enjoy this book, and find it useful for your background preparation when working with the cards.

Using This Book

There are two parts to this book….

MORE ON MEMORIZING THE CARDS
As discussed above, it can be used to help memorize
the meanings of the cards – I hope that you will find
the Aide-Mémoire: General Themes for the Minor
Arcana particularly useful. But also the Key Word
Guide for each card has been kept as short as possible
and should be easier to memorize than the sometimes
voluminous texts that appear in many Tarot books.
Just turn to the page for the card you want and you'll
see the Key Word Guide near the bottom.

USING THE ORACLE
Also, there is the Yes / No Oracle which can be used
for two different types of reading: either for a quick
one card reading; or it can be used with the Key Word
Guide to form the basis of a more detailed reading.

SINGLE CARD SPREAD
For a quick one card YES or NO answer, this book
can help. Each of the cards has a YES or NO answer
in the Oracle section for the card in question, with
qualifying text where needed. So when using the Yes /
No Oracle you may get a simple yes, or a simple no,
or there may be text with the verdict which you should
definitely take into account when giving the answer.

MULTI-CARD SPREADS
For a more detailed multi-card reading, you should use
the Key Word Guide for each card drawn in the
layout. Please bear in mind that the text in bold in

each Key Word Guide has been emphasized because it should be given weight in the reading (also it may be relevant to the motive behind the question being asked, conscious or subconscious), unless the reader gets informed by their intuitive knowing that the emphasis is not required.

Text that is both bold and underlined should be given additional weight in the reading.

Examples for the different types of reading follow:

EXAMPLES FOR A SINGLE CARD SPREAD
If you want a quick Yes / No Oracle reading on a question and for example: you draw

The Magician, upright, then the answer to the question would be "YES, however the person being read for will definitely have to pay the price that responsibility brings for their choices and actions".

However, as above, if instead you draw the *Nine of Wands, upright,* then the answer to the question would be a simple "YES". A more in depth answer using the single card would be, "YES, apply yourself to practical matters and your inner strength and passion will help you find a way through." Or, if you draw the *Nine of Wands, reversed,* then the answer to the question would be a simple "YES" again. However a more in depth answer using the single card would be "YES, but you need to find a fresh perspective if you are to make progress."

EXAMPLES OF MULTI-CARD SPREADS
For a detailed multi-card reading there are any number of possible layouts for the Oracle. Personally I tend to lay the cards intuitively, but if you prefer a set layout then I have found the following spreads to be helpful:

Converting single card to a multi-card spread
If you need more information around the single card answer you have drawn, you can convert the single card spread into a multi-card spread.

See Figure 1. for the card placements.

Figure 1.

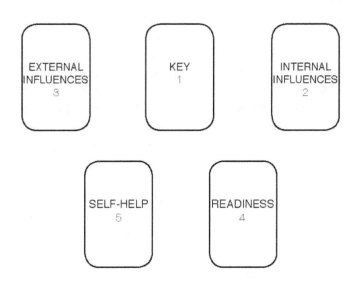

The single card that you have already drawn now becomes the Key Card for the multi-card spread. Place the Key Card in position 1.

Shuffle the deck once while asking for more information on the original question and its answer; then draw a card and place it to the right of the Key Card, in position 2. This is the Internal Influences Card (what inside the person is prompting this).

Draw the next card and place it to the left of the Key Card, in position 3. This is the External Influences Card (what outside the person is prompting this).

Draw another card and place it below the Internal

Influences Card, in position 4. This is the Readiness Card, which will comment on whether the person is ready to take on the course of action/events that relate to their question.

Draw one last card and place it under the External Influences Card, in position 5. This is the Self-Help Card, which will comment on anything that the person can do to help themselves during the unfolding events.

Remember that the outcome is already covered by the Key Card, the other cards just provide more information around that Key Card.

Situational choice spread
This spread can be used with the yes / no answers to give oracular guidance regarding your possible choices in a particular situation.

See Figure 2. for the card placements.

Figure 2.

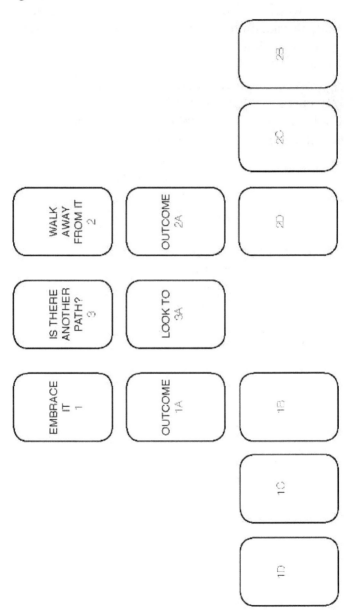

EMBRACE IT 1

IS THERE ANOTHER PATH? 3

WALK AWAY FROM IT 2

OUTCOME 1A

LOOK TO 3A

OUTCOME 2A

1B

1C

1D

2B

2C

2D

There are three possible choices covered in the spread:

The first choice would be to embrace the situation.

The second choice would be to avoid the situation by walking away from it.

And the third choice would be to look for another way to handle the situation, to find another path to travel.

Lay the cards as shown, start with card 1, next card 2, and then card 3. Then lay the next row 1a, 2a, 3a, then lay the remaining cards for choice 1: 1b, 1c, 1d, and finally the remaining cards for choice 2: 2b, 2c, and 2d.

Embrace it: choice 1.

Card 1 gives guidance on the most productive way to embrace the situation, which will likely include the approach to take, whether it asks you to present a mental, physical, emotional or creative solution/course of action (depending on the suit of the card). And whether it is something you should embrace "YES", or avoid embracing "NO" – If the answer is no, check choices 2 and 3 for alternative options.

Card 1a provides you with information on the outcome, what the initial results of embracing the situation will be.

Cards 1b, 1c, and 1d then give details on the ongoing path of evolution the outcome will take. These are things to be aware of that may have an effect on events over the longer term.

Walk away from it: choice 2.

Card 2 gives guidance on the most effective way to

avoid getting entangled in the situation, which will likely include the approach to take, whether it asks you to present a mental, physical, emotional or creative solution/course of action (depending on the suit of the card). And whether it is something you should actively avoid "YES", or in fact not avoid "NO" – If the answer is no, you should check choices 1 and 3 to see the alternative options.

Card 2a provides you with information on the outcome, what the initial results of avoiding the situation will be.

Cards 2b, 2c, and 2d then give details on the ongoing path of evolution the outcome will take. These are things to be aware of that may have an effect on events over the longer term.

Another path: choice 3.

If you don't embrace the situation, or avoid it, but instead allow events to take their own course; or alternatively you want to seek a unique or creative way of dealing with the situation. In this case, card 3 will confirm whether this is beneficial "YES" or not "NO", and what likely form this alternative path will take.

Card 3a provides information about how to find your alternative solution, where you should look in order to get guidance on finding the path ahead.

Remember, for choices 1 and 2, just because the outcome cards 1a or 2a seem to be unfavourable to you, or not what you wanted, it doesn't mean it's not the route you should take. It just means it's going to be harder work, or more emotionally challenging than you normally find comfortable.

Card 1 or card 2 will give the yes / no answer for each choice respectively, and it's that "YES" or "NO" that you should be looking at if you want to work on your life lessons as a human being.

Each of the three choices the oracle is commenting on in this spread will have their price, their lessons, and their prize. It's up to you to decide which way you want to go.

Specific question
If you have a specific question and you want a deeper answer than a straight yes or no then the following spread can give you a spiritual as well as physical Oracle: It is designed to be used with questions along the lines of, "I intend to *N*. Tell me more about it?" – Where *N* is replaced with whatever course of action it is that you want to undertake.

See Figure 3. for the card placements.

Figure 3.

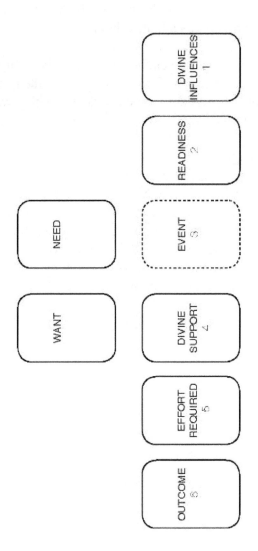

As before, shuffle the cards while concentrating on your question, and then lay the cards.

The first card to lay is the NEED card at the top, just right of centre. The second card to lay is the WANT card on the top, just left of centre. Next, beneath them, lay cards 1 through 6 in order right to left, as shown in the diagram above.

Card 3 is optional and should only be laid if it feels right to do so. If present in the spread, card 3 should be placed directly below the NEED card.

(If card 3 is not present in the spread then the space where it would have been is left blank, and what would have been card 3 becomes card 4, card 4 becomes card 5, and card 5 becomes card 6.)

Card 4 should be placed directly below the WANT card. This effectively separates the spread into two halves: on the right-hand side are the emotional, internal, spiritual cards; on the left-hand side are the more physical, external, results cards.

The NEED card. This card tells you about an inner need or life lesson that you have to come to terms with in some way, shape, or form. It speaks of something that is required for your spiritual evolution during your life time. And this inner need is something which your current intended course of action is likely to bring to the surface where your conscious mind can become aware of it.

The WANT card. This card comments on why you

want what you want, your motives and desire to achieve this thing. Are you pursuing the right goal for the right reasons?

Card 1 tells you about the form any divine influences are likely to take in order to drive you to face your need, encouraging you to deal with it.

Card 2 comments on your personal disposition with regard to this need: are you ready and willing to face this life lesson yet, or will it come as an unexpected shock?

Card 3 (if present) is about any event that affects you in order to trigger the life lesson that you need to experience. If there is a card 3 event it may have strong links with card 4 and card 6.

Card 4 is basically the "YES" or "NO" answer card, in that it explains whether your Higher Self supports the course of action you are taking in order to get your want. If there is a "NO" answer here, you would be strongly advised to rethink your goal, and how you are going about achieving it. Either, it's not what you are supposed to be doing with your life and / or you are going about it totally the wrong way; or, the time is not yet right and you would be wise to delay pursuing this goal for a while.

Card 5 will comment on the effort you are required to make in order to attain your goal.

Card 6 speaks about the outcome of your intended course of action.

In life, we frequently seem to keep coming up against the same obstacles again and again. It can be very frustrating. … With this spread, because it brings divine influence and inner need into the reading it allows you to get a glimpse of any emotional blocks, or places where your character needs work, which may be preventing you from making progress. It lets you find out why you keep tending to bump into the same obstacles time and time again. Once the inner need has been successfully addressed, or at the very least taken into account, you should then be able to set about achieving what you want in life with far fewer hindrances.

An aide-mémoire:

General Themes for the Minor Arcana

Each of the suits, and each of the numbers (Kings, Aces, Twos, etc) has a theme. Memorizing these themes can greatly help when it comes time to make your interpretation of a card if its specific meaning eludes you. Coming up blank when you turn over a card is something that happens to even the best readers once in a while. This list of themes will at least provide you with a starting point, which you can then apply to the images on the card face.

The Suit	Element	The Expression
Wands	Fire	Creativity (creativity / imagination / inspiration)
Cups	Water	Emotion (feelings / relationships / intuition)
Swords	Air	Mind (life challenges / obstacles / conflict)
Pentacles	Earth	Physical reality (material things / financial affairs)

The Cards

Ace	New beginnings, energy, a successful germination.
Two	Potential in action: the balance of opposites, the dance of yin & yang.
Three	Initial completion, achievement, an event with consequences.
Four	Stability, the reality of a situation, the brief lull after an action or event, a

	pause in activity, retreat.
Five	Change: forced by conflict or obstacles.
Six	Social balance, harmony and equality, ringing the past into the present, help or recognition from others, a solution to problems, satisfying need.
Seven	Knowledge, too many choices: decide on one goal and work towards it, *making a choice*.
Eight	Death & rebirth: regeneration, new growth, a new beginning.
Nine	A foundation: feeling the need for completion, you can make your dreams come true.
Ten	Completion of a cycle, the realization that truth abides and that work is needed to maintain success, fulfilment.
Page	The birth of the new, a wealth of potential and possibility, an infant. Male of female, female of male, emergence. Earth.
Knight	Student, adventurer, movement. (Sagittarius, Pisces, Gemini, Virgo.) Instincts and desire govern our actions in place of human judgement. You are defined by what you do in the world, not by who you are. Fire.
Queen	Knowledge, feminine need, opportunity (Leo, Scorpio, Aquarius, Taurus.) Conscious awareness expressed by the element of the suit. Water.
King	Experience, commitment, fulfilment. (Aries, Cancer, Libra, Capricorn.) Air.

THE MINOR ARCANA

Ace of Wands

ORACLE: YES – the inspiration, creativity and passion are available for you to get the ball rolling, if you choose to.

KEY WORD GUIDE:

Upright: A passionate, inspired, energetic start.
Life force. Drive.
The birth of a child.

Reversed: The outlook is good, but delays are present. Be realistic.
The need to focus your energy.

Ace of Cups

ORACLE: YES – initial passion is strong.
A note of caution: did you ask a question, or demand the answer you want?

KEY WORD GUIDE:

Upright: An upsurge of emotion. A strong initial attraction to something or someone.
Water permeates, merging.
Love affairs, engagements, marriages, births.

Reversed: Strong but troubled emotions.
Sadness. Exhaustion, anxiety, unreal expectations, disenchantment, bitterness.

Ace of Swords

ORACLE: YES – disruption and swift change
herald a chance for success.

KEY WORD GUIDE:
Upright: Necessary disruption. Swift change, a
new beginning.
Clear thinking. Cutting through
obstacles and gaining victory.

Reversed: Anxiety and stress over harsh words,
misjudgements and delays. Despite
this, there is a good chance of
success.

Ace of Pentacles

ORACLE: YES

KEY WORD GUIDE:
Upright: A financial gift or opportunity. You
have the energy and enthusiasm needed
to make something real.
A new business or career. First step
towards money.

Reversed: Insecure finances. Beware of greed:
unsound investments, & gambling.
Arguments about money.
Showing off. Throwing good money
after bad is a definite risk here.

Two of Wands

ORACLE: YES – this is a tipping point. Choose your path wisely.

KEY WORD GUIDE:

Upright: Potential. The balance between Yin and Yang.
Focused will. Knowledge with action lets you to aim for what you want.
Beneficial for property matters.

Reversed: Giving up power. Frustration due to other people.
The need to adapt or change (plans, people, etc)

Two of Cups

ORACLE: YES

KEY WORD GUIDE:

Upright: The early stages of a successful relationship: romantic or platonic. A meeting of hearts and minds.
Commitment, imagination, merging, harmony.
Any previous bad times are now over.

Reversed: Separation, jealousy – rough times ahead.

Two of Swords

ORACLE: YES – but your fears must be faced
with honesty before you can make a
beneficial decision.

KEY WORD GUIDE:
Upright: Equally powerful opposing forces.
Struggle. Balance of power.
Unresolved emotional conflict. **Your
fears must be faced with honesty,
only then can you make a decision.**

Reversed: Betrayal, indecision, averting your
eyes and missing an opportunity.
BEWARE OF FRAUD!
Resolving a difficult issue.

Two of Pentacles

ORACLE: YES – clever use of resources will keep
you solvent.
Money in equals money out.

KEY WORD GUIDE:
Upright: Juggling finances, physical action and
change. Creative solutions and clever
use of resources will keep you solvent,
just. **MONEY IN = MONEY OUT.**

Reversed: Recklessly ignoring what needs to be
done to maintain your security and
your financial welfare. Throwing away
money. Focus on the one important
task, other things can wait.

Three of Wands

ORACLE: YES – it's a start, but there's more to do.

KEY WORD GUIDE:
Upright: You've taken the first step on your journey. The goal in reality was only the beginning, you have more to do. Communication & activity. Good omen for marriage or other close union. Independence: be true to yourself.

Reversed: Delays are possible. Be patient and swallow your pride. Allow people in, it is wise to work with others at this time.

Three of Cups

ORACLE: YES – but beware of dangerous self-indulgence and casual promises.

KEY WORD GUIDE:
Upright: Celebrations, reunions, marriages, births. Emotional happiness and celebration with others. Beware of casual promises. A brief time-out from the struggle of life.

Reversed: Independence, **dangerous self-indulgence**, difficulties between friends. Lust or unrequited love consume you. Unwelcome news about relationships.

Three of Swords

ORACLE: NO

KEY WORD GUIDE:

Upright: Sorrow, pain. Unwelcome but
inevitable change releases tension. A
reality check. Harsh truth must be faced
however painful. Divorce. Surgery.
Dead wood must be trimmed before
new growth can occur.

Reversed: Strife brings stressful upheaval. But
the healing process has begun. A
release from sorrow or depression.

Three of Pentacles

ORACLE: YES

KEY WORD GUIDE:

Upright: The foundations have been laid.
Solid progress has been made, the
basic structure is sound – now you need
to add the fine detail.
Hard work, desire for mastery and
success. Positive use of skills and
talents leads to success and profit.
In business: slow, steady progress.

Reversed: Fear of failure, mediocrity, being too
conservative. In trying to please
everyone you waste your talent and
your opportunities.
Incomplete or flawed work.

Four of Wands

ORACLE: YES

KEY WORD GUIDE:
Upright: Harvest. Reaping the rewards of hard
               labour. Celebration & congratulation.
               Combined energies (people) working
               together, the result is abundance.
               Creativity and stability combine to
               bring prosperity. Artistic excellence.
               Setting up a new home or buying a
               property.

Reversed: Organization is lacking, people can't
               work together. Temporary restriction
               leads to feelings of frustration, and
               despondence; but good news is on
               the way and things will improve.

Four of Cups

ORACLE: NO – if you ignore what you have and
               the opportunities presented how will
               anything come of them?

KEY WORD GUIDE:
Upright: **If you ignore opportunities nothing
               will come of them.**
               Lack of enthusiasm. Discontent.
               Apathy, boredom, restlessness.
               Desire for change – versus – loss
               through inaction: you choose which.
               In love: passivity diminishes the
               energy & excitement.

Reversed:	Prevention of loss. Make a decision, take action.
	Deep inner need – fear of loss.
	Follow your dreams to that longed for goal, it's time to set about making it happen.

Four of Swords

ORACLE: YES - the time is right to take a rest and recuperate.

KEY WORD GUIDE:

Upright:	A time for rest, recuperation and relaxation. The need to recharge mentally, physically and emotionally: **take a timeout**. Information, knowledge and solutions will come while you rest. Problems may solve themselves.
	Individuality, discovering your Higher Self, awakening to spirit.
Reversed:	Becoming more involved. Taking action.
	Information that prompts you to respond.
	Exile. Forced confinement. Adverse effects of being alone. Illness.
	If you have reached your limits, nervous exhaustion enforces complete rest.

Four of Pentacles

ORACLE: YES

KEY WORD GUIDE:

Upright: Material stability, holding on to your possessions. Fear of loss.
Hidden insecurity, fear of emotional pain.
Achievement, goals are fulfilled.
Financial problems will be overcome and you will retain your profits, as well as gain more in the future.
A materialistic attitude.

Reversed: A lack of concern for material possessions. Letting go of things.
Additional effort and study are required if tests are to be passed.
Greed, covetousness, envy of the prosperity of others.
A short delay in the payment of debts.

Five of Wands

ORACLE: NO – the normal route will not be effective. Are you aiming too high?

KEY WORD GUIDE:

Upright: **Struggle and frustration, competition and challenges. The normal route will not be effective.** The need to come up with creative solutions to the problems that face you. You are up to the job, despite your doubts.
Harsh reality, obstacles and limitations. The use of creative energy to break down anything that is static, dull or limiting. **Beware of aiming too high.** Dealing with contractual obligations.

Reversed: A dispute becomes more serious. Feeling stressed. Trust is an issue. Bitterness, anger and feelings of betrayal erupt over petty things. Worrying about legal or work matters, read the small print.

Five of Cups

ORACLE: NO – you are placing too much emphasis on your pain.
This is opportunity disguised as loss, a chance to come to terms with things as they are and make a fresh start.

KEY WORD GUIDE:

Upright: Emotional distress. **<u>Sorrow, loss,
regret.</u>** Too much emphasis is being
placed on the loss. **The important
things in life are still left, if you take
a look: family, self-respect, hope.**
Coming to terms with irrevocable loss.
Revenge and wallowing are unhealthy.
This is your chance to head out to new
pastures. Use it.

Reversed: Understanding, appreciation for what
remains, fresh hope for something
new.
You have gained far more than you
have lost. Disappointment won't last,
unhappiness soon passes.

Five of Swords

ORACLE: NO

KEY WORD GUIDE:

Upright: A harsh situation: defeat, shame,
humiliation, loss. Emotional betrayal.
Your perspective is skewed, you can't
think clearly or focus, so don't trust
what your mind or senses tell you.
A particular situation is no longer
workable or salvageable. Any battles
fought to sustain it will be lost. Accept
the inevitable, cut your losses and get
out before you cause yourself genuine
pain and suffering.

Reversed:	Speak up, defend yourself. Refuse to accept defeat. An unconventional solution to obstacles is possible.
	OR:
	Defeat is inevitable, but you will find it easier to cut your losses and walk away. Desire to fight verses a realistic assessment of the obstacles you face.

Five of Pentacles

ORACLE: NO

KEY WORD GUIDE:

Upright:	Financial trouble, loss: stress. Pay careful attention to your health. Remain open and flexible; help is available from someone who has experienced hardship.
	Rash and ill-thought out action may cause more problems than it solves. Romance may still blossom if you don't allow stress to quash it – love doesn't cost money.
Reversed:	Loss of cash could have been avoided if you had paid more attention to financial details. Take a proper look at your situation: now is the time to change, and take firm action to solve the problems you have caused yourself. Your attitude to money must become realistic.

Six of Wands

ORACLE: YES

KEY WORD GUIDE:
Upright: You have been recognized and publicly
               acclaimed for your success. [Take note
               of the passions, attitudes and actions
               that led you to success.] Confidence,
               optimism and self-belief. Productivity.
               Victorious aftermath. Overcoming the
               odds.

Reversed: Disquiet, doubt, pessimism, creative
               blocks. Obstacles to success can be
               overcome with patience, victory can
               be yours. If you push for success you
               will waste energy and time. Relax
               and allow it to happen.

Six of Cups

ORACLE: YES – but is dwelling on the past
               hindering you or helping you?

KEY WORD GUIDE:
Upright: Past memories, nostalgia. Memory
               blurred by emotion or sentiment.
               <u>Losing yourself in what was.</u>
               A time of gentleness and serenity.
               An old friend returns.
               If you are faced with a problem the
               answer lies in the past, or with your
               ancestors who have been through the
               same.

Reversed:	Do not let the past rule your life: now is what counts.
	Look ahead to what needs to be done.
	Outdated methods, ideas and assumptions prevent you from moving forwards.
	Fantasy and dreams have intruded on to your memories of what really happened: strip away the illusions, find the reality.

Six of Swords

ORACLE: YES

KEY WORD GUIDE:

Upright:	You can leave the storms behind you: either by moving job, house, country – or by thinking your way to a solution. Agreeable solutions are possible, calm lies ahead. Instead of rocking the boat hold your tongue, avoid rubbing your victory into the wounds of others.
	Travel. "Crossing water".
	Ideas; puzzle solving. Separating mind from emotion.
Reversed:	Seeing the problems in grand ideas, but the delays and minor problems are only temporary.
	A journey will help you escape, so you can deal with your emotions in a calmer environment. Put some distance between you and the issue, it will help clear your head.

Six of Pentacles

ORACLE: YES – but only need is satisfied, not want. Avoid waste.

KEY WORD GUIDE:

Upright: Financial aid: charity, gifts, generosity, appreciation. Your situation may feel dire, but help is at hand from other people. Tighten your belt and be grateful for the help others give you. Enough money will be found or borrowed to solve the immediate problem – but there will not be any extra. **Need is satisfied, not want. (Save for a rainy day.)**

Reversed: Wasting good fortune. Extravagant spending in order to maintain a lie. Money is spent like water.
Feelings of separation from others. Inequalities between people.
Helping other people may drain your resources.
Carelessness will cost you.

Seven of Wands

ORACLE: YES – but focused effort is required.

KEY WORD GUIDE:

Upright: A choice forced by passion: the need to make a decision or take the initiative. Focused effort is required.
A deeper understanding of self: a change in profession.
Competition or obstacles need to be overcome if you are to maintain your leadership and succeed.

Reversed: Self-confidence may be an issue. You can succeed if you can stay out of your own way.
Talk to others and be ready for fast remedial action if things go awry.

Seven of Cups

ORACLE: YES – you need to make a choice and then apply the work required to bring that choice into reality.

KEY WORD GUIDE:

Upright: Many ideas, dreams, wishes. **<u>The need to make a choice and apply the work to bring that choice into reality.</u>**
Trust your gut and go with your instincts when making the decision.
The Veil lies between you and concrete reality: this is a test of focus and practical application.

Reversed: Putting dreams into action. Realism.
             Assessing what needs to be done to
             create something solid.
             Wishful thinking may lead you down
             false paths. Selfish indulgence in
             negative emotion: lust, alcohol.

Seven of Swords

ORACLE: NO – you need to define yourself and
               your position, find your centre.
               Deception is likely, obstacles block
               your way.

KEY WORD GUIDE:

Upright: Your thoughts are all over the place;
             you feel splintered within yourself –
             either unconnected or conflicted.
             **"Unstable Effort"; <u>the need to define
             yourself and your position.</u>
             Deception is likely. Obstacles block
             your way.** Nothing is as it seems: lies
             and betrayal, or callousness obscure the
             reality of the situation and cause you
             pain.

Reversed: Clearing away obstacles. Effort is
             rewarded.
             Avoid any kind of dishonesty.
             Legal or contractual agreements will
             not be favourable to you.
             Malice and deliberate deception; lies
             and theft are very likely. Your
             property is at risk.

Seven of Pentacles

ORACLE: YES – there is a choice to make. And
consider this, if a task is soul
destroying perhaps you are in the
wrong line of work?

KEY WORD GUIDE:

Upright: A choice between the tried and tested
methods, or a new course of action.
The important thing is the work itself
and what it produces. You need to find
clarity: the work may be flawed. Keep
at it. Slow, steady progress leads to
eventual success.

Reversed: If you hold back from commitment to
the task at hand, then no matter how
hard you work, you won't gain a
sense of satisfaction from the results.
**If a task is soul-destroying,
perhaps you are in the wrong line
of work?**
Avoid lending money at this time.

Eight of Wands

ORACLE: YES

KEY WORD GUIDE:

Upright: Creative passion: the desire for
            expansion and regeneration. It is time
            to move forwards; action, "Swiftness"
            and activity bring great productivity.
            Many possibilities, you can do all of
            them if you plan well, there's no need
            to choose one over another.

Reversed: Delays, confusion, frustration, the
            need to make a choice. Poor
            communication, misunderstandings,
            missed phone calls. Meetings fall
            through.
            Avoid being rude and do not commit
            your views to writing – you could
            offend the wrong person.

Eight of Cups

ORACLE: YES – reality needs to be faced.

KEY WORD GUIDE:

Upright: "Abandoned Success." Something you
            used to care about a lot no longer
            seems important, or you've been forced
            to abandon it. It is time to move on,
            follow your heart to the next phase in
            your life. Onwards & upwards.
            Emotional regeneration is underway.

Reversed: Stability is emphasized; you need to
              see the value in what you have and
              resist the urge to move on.
              Pursuing fantasy, or running away
              from problems, or refusing to face-up
              to reality is a *big* mistake.

Eight of Swords

ORACLE: YES – but you need to keep a level
              head, think clearly and take appropriate
              action in order to find a solution to this
              difficult and challenging situation.

KEY WORD GUIDE:

Upright: Events may seem beyond your control
              but you are the one who has the power
              to change things. A new attitude or
              approach may be required. Perhaps you
              need to ask for help?
              Frustration, difficulty, bad luck – but
              solutions are there if you look for them.
              **The need to keep a level head, think
              clearly and take appropriate action
              in a difficult and challenging
              situation.**

Reversed: Seeing things clearly. The frustration
              is almost unbearable. If you take
              your irritation or anger out on
              innocent bystanders you will pay for
              it, one way or another.

Eight of Pentacles

ORACLE: YES

KEY WORD GUIDE:

Upright: The need to retrain. The process of creating a more rewarding and meaningful life. Choosing to study: the skills and knowledge gained, will help you in your future career. Personal satisfaction, and future profit.

Reversed: Impatience, you want it all and you want it now, and you want it to be perfect.
Perhaps you are being forced to work at, or learn, something you find dull and unrewarding. If so, you need to make a change in your career or course of study – even if the prospect is scary.

Nine of Wands

ORACLE: YES

KEY WORD GUIDE:

Upright: The need for creativity or passion. Your resilience will help you overcome all opposition. The practical application of learned wisdom; a single piece of knowledge changes a situation dramatically. Inner strength, you are in a place of safety, liberation.

Reversed: Confusion. Obstinate and inflexible attitudes will only confine you. Misguided attitudes. You need a fresh way of looking at the situation if you are to make progress.

Nine of Cups

ORACLE: YES

KEY WORD GUIDE:

Upright: The need for emotion and intuition. "Joy". A heartfelt dream may come true if you apply yourself to achieving it. A time to pursue pleasure and sensual satisfaction. Celebration, entertainment, joy: treasure the precious moments.

Reversed: Neglecting the feelings and needs of
              others. Arrogance, selfishness,
              possessiveness, vanity, cloying
              sentimentality, a fickle attitude.
              Frustration, thinking you deserve
              more.

Nine of Swords

ORACLE: YES – you must be honest with
              yourself in the face of harsh truth.
              Things may be dark and depressing
              right now, but you will find a way
              through. There is hope.

KEY WORD GUIDE:

Upright: The need for courage, thought and
              decisive action. This is a painful time
              for you. Beset by inner demons: fear,
              suffering, anxiety, but you will not
              flinch or look away. **Honesty in the
              face of harsh truth.** A refusal to give
              in. You will not bow to the
              expectations of others. **Dark times and
              depression: but you will find a way
              through.**

Reversed: Self-punishment, feelings of guilt. But
              the situation is not hopeless; your
              torment is nearly over.
              Turning away, retreat, avoiding a
              painful situation.

Nine of Pentacles

ORACLE: YES – but hard work and serious
thought are needed to make your
financial situation secure. Anything
you gain will depend on how you've
nurtured it: as you have sowed, so shall
you reap.

KEY WORD GUIDE:
Upright: The need for physical and financial
security. Prosperity.
A period of calm, contentment and
enjoyment brought about by a sense of
financial security. But **hard work and
serious thought is needed to make
your financial situation secure.**
Money is an issue: either money gained
or money spent freely without thought
of the consequences. **Inheritance (as
you have sowed so shall you reap),**
receiving unexpected news.

Reversed: You are concerned about the future,
so you are careful to hold on to
money or preserve what you can.
Being obliged to sell possessions in
order to pay off heavy debts.
A financial venture you thought was
promising tanks.
A life of comfort based on theft, or
the misery of others.

Ten of Wands

ORACLE: YES – but you need to pick the most important task and complete that first.

KEY WORD GUIDE:
Upright: Dedication brings stress: heavy burdens. Desire, belief, passion. Hard work and prioritizing your responsibilities brings success. You can't do everything at once, **pick the most important task and complete that first.**

Reversed: Doubt and a failure to believe in your own abilities; you allow other people to convince you that you are wasting your time. They have their own agendas and your welfare is not their priority. Additional tasks and pressure from others is an unnecessary burden.

Ten of Cups

ORACLE: YES

KEY WORD GUIDE:
Upright: Family unity, contentment, lasting happiness. You have reached a point where you enjoy life, and understand the work required to achieve and maintain love, peace, contentment.

Reversed: Look past the momentary
             frustrations, there is joy here if you
             search for it. Some close
             acquaintances depart, but new
             friends arrive to take their place.

Ten of Swords

ORACLE: YES – whatever is at an end
               (relationship, job, life at home?) is over
               because it is no longer valid.

KEY WORD GUIDE:
Upright: "Ruin". An ending opens the way for a
               new beginning.
               **Whatever is at an end – relationship,
               job, life at home – is over because it
               is no longer valid.** It could be a very
               painful experience if you have not been
               honest with yourself. You may feel
               betrayed, ruined, abandoned. In fact
               this is a positive opportunity to
               transcend emotion, see the full pattern,
               discover truth, and move on.

Reversed: Confusion, flawed vision, worry:
             there are a few more trials to
             overcome before the rise back into
             the light. Do not give in to despair,
             you will bounce back.

Ten of Pentacles

ORACLE: YES

KEY WORD GUIDE:

Upright: Wealth, inheritance, family traditions.
                Putting in the hard work to bring a crop
                to harvest: making solid foundations
                for now and the future. Creating a
                legacy.
                Marriage. Excellent business prospects.
                Wealth.

Reversed: Family disputes over finances,
                squabbles over inheritance rights.
                Divorce and the resulting division of
                assets.
                Traditions stifle your future
                prospects. Black sheep: leaving the
                safety net, looking for a new start.

Page of Wands

ORACLE: YES

KEY WORD GUIDE:

Upright: Inspiration with great potential, nurture
                and protect it. "Mighty oaks from little
                acorns grow".
                Enthusiasm, the uninhibited energy of
                youth. A message. A traveller.

Reversed: A spoiled brat stirs up trouble. Bad
                news.
                Dyslexia or problems with study.
                Laziness.
                Exhaustion. Holding back feelings.

Page of Cups

ORACLE: YES

KEY WORD GUIDE:

Upright: New emotions: love, the birth of a
                child, a change of heart. The first
                glimmering of intuition; unformed
                ideas.
                Emotion creates form, which will
                dissipate if it is not contained: practical
                matters need to be attended to.
                Gentleness. Merging.
                A boyish girl, a girlish boy. Osmosis.

Reversed: Finding self-identity; you have the
             chance to think more clearly and
             make decisions, or speak to others,
             about the situation now.
             Idleness, fantasy – someone is living
             in a dream world, possibly trivial
             attitudes. This person will not be
             pleased when reality conflicts with,
             and bursts, their bubble.

Page of Swords

ORACLE: YES – but any detachment you think
             you have is self-delusion. Your current
             behaviour and decisions are rooted in
             emotion, so stop kidding yourself.

KEY WORD GUIDE:

Upright: Shallow conversations: learning how to
             interact with others. From this, deeper
             connections may follow.
             New ideas that need attention and time
             if they are to grow into something
             workable.
             Legal disputes. Malicious trickery and
             slander from others. Anxiety.
             **Your behaviour and decisions stem
             from desire or fear, not objectivity:
             detachment is self-delusion.**

Reversed: Being aware of your motives and
             acting on instinct. Any suspicion or
             nervousness has cause; someone
             clever, manipulative, and vengeful is
             attempting to get even over a past
             slight – either real or imagined.

Page of Pentacles

ORACLE: YES

KEY WORD GUIDE:

Upright: A small beginning from which concrete achievement is possible: the opportunity for material success. Laying a foundation, hard work and diligence is required. Studying or experiencing the natural world. A serious, thoughtful youth may help you start a project.

Reversed: An impatient, whimsical, easily distracted youth who constantly wants money. Self-indulgence is the primary concern of this person: to them cost is meaningless.

Knight of Wands

ORACLE: YES – a positive *can-do* attitude will take you far.

KEY WORD GUIDE:
Upright: Passion, imagination, energy and action. Confidence can lead to reckless action that frequently is successful – if not, you pick yourself up and dive in to your next project. A positive attitude. Changes are occurring: perhaps you will move house, job or country? Impatience. Quick decisions.

Reversed: You've been too impulsive, and taken a lot of risks that leave you exposed. Someone else's promises mean nothing. Disillusionment, the loss of idealism.
Someone with a fiery nature who thrives on rivalry and feuds: envy, jealousy, conflict.

Knight of Cups

ORACLE: YES

KEY WORD GUIDE:
Upright: A lover or good friend arrives. It is a good time to pursue your dreams, or follow your intuition.
The inner turmoil of a waterfall. Your dreams conflict with the pressures and responsibilities of every day life.

Reversed:	A good looking but unpleasant or deceiving lover will soon depart. You want to indulge in your dreamy and introverted side, so you resent the demands people place on you.

Knight of Swords

ORACLE:	YES – but you can not predict events or how people will react.

KEY WORD GUIDE:

Upright:	Disruption, chaos, welcome change: a butterfly flaps its wings. **<u>Unpredictable events or reactions from others.</u>** A stimulating, fun person who flits about in search of entertainment. Boredom may lead you to a quest for education or a career change. Intellect, force and charm: a warrior who speeds through your life like a summer storm.
Reversed:	Brashness, throwing caution to the wind, going too far. Your behaviour attracts trouble, and you have no staying power. A clever liar enters your life: they are very convincing, yet secretive and treacherous, they always have an excuse or alibi, and they have a tendency to violence.

Knight of Pentacles

ORACLE: YES

KEY WORD GUIDE:

Upright: Patience, hard work, dedication and perseverance (seeing it through right to the end) lead to success. Progress is slow but steady. Making something material and lasting.

Good news in financial and business dealings.

A responsible person who does not take many risks: they are hard working, serious and trustworthy. They are passionate about what they do and will see things through to the end despite any painful struggle or setbacks they endure.

Reversed: Compromise. Being realistic about the situation.

Do not believe the promises made, this person is greedy and will end up costing you money.

Avoid travel in relation to business, or any unnecessary financial spending.

Queen of Wands

ORACLE: YES

KEY WORD GUIDE:

Upright: A powerful woman who is passionate
                and creative. She hates losing so she
                doesn't take risks, she knows her
                limits.
                Organization, knowledge, skill.
                Warmth, generosity, strength,
                optimism. A sense of joy in life.
                Astonishment: a lucky break – seize the
                opportunity with both hands.

Reversed: A dictator: negative, jaded, vengeful,
                possessive; hates independence in
                others, bad tempered, envious. This
                person needs shaking up.

Queen of Cups

ORACLE: YES – find your centre and allow your
                intuition to guide you.

KEY WORD GUIDE:

Upright: Mysticism, intuition, emotion. Follow
                your gut instinct.
                Mystery, seduction, charisma: for you
                or about you.
                A deep pool: unfathomable, receptive
                and reflective. Water of water.
                A psychic, an artist, someone who
                knows love.

Reversed: Fear of love. Uncertainty. Dwelling in romantic fantasy.
              A false lover. Someone who uses the appearance of frailty or weakness to manipulate others. This person is vain, deceitful, and demands their whims are satisfied; they are a drain on emotions and finances of others.

Queen of Swords

ORACLE: YES – but the solution to the problem is not the one you currently have in mind. Keep thinking and you'll find it.

KEY WORD GUIDE:

Upright: An intense and painful problem can be overcome if you concentrate on achieving your goal. **The solution to the problem is not the one you currently have in mind. Keep thinking and you'll find it.**
              Remaining calm in the face of danger, knowledge can save you. Courage, idealism: hiding emotions or suffering. A woman who loves knowledge: intelligent, logical, and very perceptive. Do not underestimate her abilities.

Reversed: A dangerous person who lives by strict and inflexible rules; they are jealous, cruel, malicious, and manipulative. As a negotiator, this person will stir up trouble by lying or by being economical with the truth. Emotional turmoil.

Queen of Pentacles

ORACLE: YES – however, if finances are causing you anxiety, make sure your decisions are based on sound judgement rather than fear.

KEY WORD GUIDE:

Upright: Someone who enjoys the physicality of life, and is willing to work hard in order to indulge their desires. Practical application of knowledge in the real world.
Generosity: a need for good food, beauty, sensuality – and sharing this with others. Nurturing and fertility.
<u>Finances may be causing you anxiety.</u>

Reversed: A need for activities involving other people: sociability, expressing yourself, contact.
You may be temporarily short of cash.
Someone stuck in their ways who loathes change. They love having money and fear losing it so they can appear to be a suspicious, mistrustful skinflint. If you are in a dispute with them over money or possessions they won't play fair, either due to greed or insecurity.

King of Wands

ORACLE: YES

KEY WORD GUIDE:

Upright: A charismatic leader: inspirational,
                creative, active, positive, ambitious but
                also restless – he hates responsibility
                and the burdens others put on him.
                An honourable, trustworthy, passionate
                gentleman.
                Creative, artistic or theatrical projects
                come to fulfilment.
                Fatherhood. Conception.

Reversed: A domineering bully: arrogant,
                bigoted, and yet charming. This
                person is very selfish, their desires
                and passions come first. Any advice
                given by this person is based
                squarely on self-interest.

King of Cups

ORACLE: YES – but you have the experience and
                intuition to find your own solutions,
                search inside for the answer.

KEY WORD GUIDE:

Upright: Your tranquillity is disturbed. Your
                outer calm hides inner turmoil. **You
                have the experience and intuition to
                find your own solutions, search
                inside for the answer.**
                A strong desire for involvement with

others, but a fear of the closeness and intimacy involved.

A charismatic man who is warm-hearted, responsible, loyal, and sensitive. He is resilient only because he has experienced and survived emotional traumas in the past. His calm is an act, a protective mask.

Reversed: Emotional upheaval, to the point where calm can not be maintained. Emotional pain, feelings of weakness. A vulnerable person who uses secrecy as protection.
An addictive personality: alcohol, drugs, gambling.

King of Swords

ORACLE: YES – but you need to seek out a fair and just solution, taking into account the needs of others as well as the rules.

KEY WORD GUIDE:
Upright: Take charge of events and use your willpower to gain control of your life. **<u>You need to seek out a fair and just solution, taking into account the needs of others as well as the rules.</u>** A time for thinking and organization. Trying to maintain social harmony via reason & quick thinking. Maintaining an empire is hard work, don't let painful experience from the past cloud your judgement.

Reversed: You are dealing with someone who is prone to suspicion and manipulation, a player of mind-games: they may be a liar or confidence trickster.
Hypocrisy: critical and extremely judgemental, yet ignoring faults or flaws in themselves.
Dogma and aggression are used to control others.

King of Pentacles

ORACLE: YES – with determination and hard work you can make it happen.

KEY WORD GUIDE:

Upright: **Determination to succeed and hard work leads to success.** Beneficial influences in business and finance. Someone calm, stable and honest who appreciates what they have, and who understands what it took to earn it.
A wealthy man who is in touch with his kingdom; he walks the land, talks to his people: a man of the earth.

Reversed: The desire for new horizons, risk or stimulation, especially in business or work.
A person who is unimaginative, greedy, corrupt and mean. They hang out with gamblers or dishonest people. This person does not wish you well – they want to possess what you have.

THE MAJOR ARCANA

The Fool

ORACLE: YES – follow your own path.

KEY WORD GUIDE:

Upright: The start of a journey, a new life path
          you wouldn't miss for all the world.
          Follow your instincts.
          Bravery born of innocence and naivety;
          your confidence brings safety.
          Doing something just for you – other
          people may think you're mad, but they
          aren't you.
          Going your own way.

Reversed: Pause for a moment and look at
          yourself. If you are behaving in an
          immature and irrational manner, then
          any whim or impulse that you follow
          could lead you into trouble or worse.
          Stop and think!

The Magician

ORACLE: YES – however you will definitely have to pay the price that responsibility brings for your choices and actions.

KEY WORD GUIDE:

Upright: The energy, potential and opportunity you need are there. Choose your path. You have the power to create your reality. **<u>Responsibility and its price.</u>**

Reversed: Liars and confidence tricksters surround you. New ventures will fail, or are purely designed to part you from your cash. **Free will, the downside: you pay the price for your decisions.**

The High Priestess

ORACLE: NO – you do not have all the facts yet,
be patient.

KEY WORD GUIDE:

Upright: A light illuminates that which was
hidden from you.
**You do not yet have all the facts, be
patient.** You know that study is
required. Someone, who keeps her
secrets.
Wisdom cannot be forced. Follow your
intuition.

Reversed: Passion may overrule common sense.
Secrets may be unwisely revealed.
Look to yourself, not others' opinions
– do not allow yourself to be lead.
If you are being passive, take action
to regain your power.

The Empress

ORACLE: YES

KEY WORD GUIDE:

Upright: Motherhood, fertility. The creativity of earth.
Abundance. Success. Satisfaction with your achievements.
Feminine earthy passion. Emotional support, emotional security.
The full moon.

Reversed: Smothering, tyranny, emotional blackmail.
Poor finances.
Doubts about your abilities may lead to detaching yourself, in order to gain some emotional distance, which in turn will allow you the space you feel you need to think things through.

The Emperor

ORACLE: YES – but your actions and decisions can be viewed as repressive by others.

KEY WORD GUIDE:

Upright: Energy, power and influence to change the environment in your favour. Law and order, structure. Fatherhood. Changing house or job. Better times ahead.
Your activity can be viewed as repressive by others.

Reversed: Tyranny. The rule of will. There is the potential for abusive behaviour.
A position of weakness; others are not trustworthy, they work against you. You find out who is pulling the strings.

The Hierophant

ORACLE: YES – conventional tradition is the
correct route.

KEY WORD GUIDE:

Upright: Spiritual quest: the search for inner
meaning and purpose in life. A bridge
between worlds who facilitates
communication. Received teaching.
Inspired wisdom. **Conventional
tradition is the correct route.**
Contractual obligations. Marriage.
Social pressure to conform.

Reversed: Unorthodox approach. Hidebound
tradition holds you back, so think for
yourself, make your own way.
You may have a crisis of faith. If so,
you need to discover your beliefs for
yourself.
Reject bad advice, whoever it comes
from!

The Lovers

ORACLE: YES – it's your choice, pick your consequences.

KEY WORD GUIDE:
Upright: A choice between one or the other. Duty verses desire. Think carefully, but follow your heart and your gut, NOT your head. Responsibility of choice: you make your own bed. Becoming an individual, an adult. Love or passion consumes you. The merging of opposites.

Reversed: Rebellion or opposition between people. Difficulty in relationships. Dissatisfaction with things as they are.
A lack of the commitment and of the courage to make a necessary choice. Adherence to duty blights your chances for happiness.

The Chariot

ORACLE: YES – unity of purpose is required, get single-minded.

KEY WORD GUIDE:

Upright: **<u>Focus is required to attain victory</u>.**
Differing forces, thoughts, emotions must be pulled together in order to drive forwards or make progress. Scattered parts united to meet one goal. Mind over matter. Self control comes first; you create your reality. Success, power, fame are all possible future outcomes if you focus your effort now. A vehicle.

Reversed: Arrogance and ego. Delays, obstacles, bad temper, doubts, weakening will. You are your own worst enemy. Relax, chill-out, de-stress.
Working with others.
Travel plans will go awry.

Strength

ORACLE: YES

KEY WORD GUIDE:

Upright: Inner courage and self discipline.
                Controlling urges and the savage, base
                instincts. Strength of character, doing
                the right thing.
                Female power: gentle persuasion,
                rather than brute force. Taming the
                savage heart.
                Tenacity, endurance, self-belief.
                Rapid recovery.
                A woman's ability to conceive.

Reversed: Feelings of weakness. Losing your
                nerve when victory is in sight, but
                success is still possible. You need to
                act or speak more directly.
                Check your motives. Are you abusing
                a position of power? Or, could you be
                pursuing the wrong goal?

The Hermit

ORACLE: YES – search for wisdom before you
act.

KEY WORD GUIDE:

Upright: Be cautious, withdraw from the
situation and think things through
carefully. Any delays are there to give
you a chance to examine your motives
and inner needs.
Time to yourself. Patience, prudence,
inner truth.
<u>The search for wisdom.</u>

Reversed: Becoming involved with others, and
being more active in the world.
If you feel isolated or lonely, now is
the time to remedy the situation.
They say "Fools rush in….": don't
"throw the baby out with the bath
water" just because you are
impatient, or think you know
everything you need to know. The
tried and tested ways of doing things
are there for a reason.

The Wheel of Fortune

ORACLE: YES

KEY WORD GUIDE:

Upright: Your fortunes are improving. A stroke
                  of luck. Circumstances are changing,
                  events take place on their own without
                  conscious control. Karma is taking an
                  active part in your life, what comes
                  around goes around. In other words,
                  life is what you make it: free will
                  verses Fate.
                  You have paved the way for this, so
                  enjoy the good times while they last,
                  and remember to save for the future.

Reversed: Seize your destiny, just remember
                  Karma is active here. Unpleasant
                  surprises could blindside you.
                  Rapid changes in luck and fortune
                  may confuse you; the constant ups
                  and downs won't last forever.

Justice

ORACLE: YES – think things through carefully. What is right, what is wrong?

KEY WORD GUIDE:

Upright: Use logic and cool intellect to find a solution. A sense of justice, of right and wrong. You are challenged to look honestly at yourself. The desire for a fair outcome.
Contracts and legal issues find in your favour – if it is fair and just.
Bodes well for marriage or a business partnership.
Balance, fairness, equilibrium.

Reversed: Dishonesty, oppression, prejudice or misinformation will be detrimental to you. An unfair outcome or situation. Are you being honest with yourself? Keep cool, and think things through carefully from every angle or the forces ranged against you will prevail. Legal difficulties: avoid contracts or legal disputes at this time.

The Hanged Man

ORACLE: YES – you will enjoy the process, and learn a lot, so do it. However, the end result won't be what you want.

KEY WORD GUIDE:

Upright: **You will enjoy the process, so do it. But the outcome you originally craved is likely to be a bust.** Joyful sacrifice. The experience and new perspective gained makes it worthwhile. A karmic debt needs to be repaid. Patience, grin and bear it; a rapid learning curve – and the lessons will benefit you.

Reversed: Responding to social pressure, rather than following your own values. Feelings of guilt. Being emotionally blackmailed. Misguided self-blame or masochism. Remove these influences so that you can move on.

Death

ORACLE: YES – illusions are stripped away by Fate.

KEY WORD GUIDE:

Upright: Great change. The transformation and growth is necessary, but probably painful. – Outdated attitudes, job, home, relationships, etc., must be left behind as your illusions are stripped away by Fate. This is the completion of one cycle and the start of the next. Death, but also the new life that will replace that which has passed.

Reversed: You may fear the change that faces you and desperately want to hold on to what was, even though you know it is over. But this situation really is over and the break up is final. However, you do have some control, despite this, and can decide when it will end and how.
It's time to move on to something new.

Temperance

ORACLE: YES – moderation and harmony with
others is the key to happiness.

KEY WORD GUIDE:
Upright: **<u>Moderation and harmony with
others is the key to happiness.</u>**
A feeling of being looked after by the
universe. Take care of yourself, be a bit
more moderate; things will improve.
Harmonious relationships. Sharing.
Cooperation. You have the opportunity
to discuss your real feelings. Calmness.
Containment. Transformation.
Explosive opposites interact peacefully;
the sanctuary of middle ground.
Negotiations are possible.

Reversed: Excess: your lower nature dominates,
extreme emotions or actions; being
uncentred, you lose sight of yourself.
Avoid places and people that are bad
for you.
Confrontation, opposition, corruption,
self-indulgence. The future results of
this will be unpleasant.

The Devil

ORACLE: NO – repression. An immovable object in your path.

KEY WORD GUIDE:

Upright: Tyranny, **repression**, slavery. Direct confrontation will NOT work. Greed, lust, addiction, destructive habits. **An immovable object in your path.** Lateral thinking and cunning are required if you want to get around this. You fail to take account of the destructive consequences of your actions or inaction. Question your motives, let go of your fear: you now have the chance to rectify a situation you created.

Reversed: Liberation. A moment of clarity and understanding. Things are brought to light.
Change your behaviour and speech from destructive to benign and you will be pleasantly surprised by the way it improves your life.
You have the chance to free yourself from the influence of people who are detrimental to you, or to give up any addictions or bad habits that have been blighting your life.

The Tower

ORACLE: NO – a harsh awakening. Disruption clarifies your situation.

KEY WORD GUIDE:

Upright: Divine intervention blows apart your safe life and what you previously believed to be true. **A sudden, disruptive, disturbing experience that forces you to reassess your situation, your attitudes and your beliefs.**
Ultimately liberating, The Tower provides the inspiration for growth and a new start; it shatters illusions and highlights values that no longer hold meaning. Pure inspiration, a harsh awakening.

Reversed: Going against the status quo. You feel the need to rebel against the restrictions that are placed on you. An awakening to the false accusations and social oppression that surrounds you. Rocking the boat.

The Star

ORACLE: YES

KEY WORD GUIDE:

Upright: Inspiration, hope, optimism, the renewal of energy. Selflessness. An outpouring of emotion. Restoration of fertility. Good health, luck, new opportunities. Problems will be solved, life will become easier.
A spring; the water of life. Possibly the awakening to spirit.

Reversed: Prospects are good, but a negative attitude prevails. Holding back, damming up emotions. Blocking yourself unnecessarily. Despite a pessimistic or cynical attitude luck will strike, a new door is about to open. It's up to you to take advantage of it.

The Moon

ORACLE: YES – you are on the right path, even if it doesn't look like it. Avoid making decisions, allow events to take their course.

KEY WORD GUIDE:

Upright: Take nothing for granted – you are in the twilight world of dreams. Emotion clouds judgement. **Avoid making quick or firm decisions at this time, instead allow events to take their course. <u>You are on the right path, even if it seems beset with briars.</u>** Confusion, uncertainty, volatile emotion, a world of shadows – nothing is clear – this leads to frustration. Let go of your goals and aims, and just be, experience the trip. Surrender to the strangeness & animal instinct. Imagination, creativity, giving desire concrete form.
In relationships: commitments will not work out. In business: financial deception, mistreatment.

Reversed: If you feel anxious about lies and insincerity, you have good reason. You want to ignore your instincts, but that would be unwise. Your emotional response to this distressing betrayal unsettles you.
Are you in a clandestine love affair? If so, you will be found out.

The Sun

ORACLE: YES

KEY WORD GUIDE:

Upright: Enthusiasm, clarity, a positive attitude. Joy, simplicity, innocence, strength, individuality. Good health, romance, good news about children.
The Higher Self in action: the truth revealed in the light of day, all deception is banished. Motives are revealed. Illusions vanish.
Success, your achievements are applauded. A happy ending.

Reversed: Good news and a pleasant surprise are on the way. This luck may go to your head. Try to avoid arrogance. There will still be some struggle, possibly a delay, but the joy and happiness you feel will remain.

Judgement

ORACLE: YES – your motives and handling of a situation will have a direct bearing on its outcome.

KEY WORD GUIDE:

Upright: <u>**Your motives and handling of a situation will have a direct bearing on its outcome.**</u> Resolution and resurrection. You are your own judge. A time of great and positive change that is both an ending and a beginning. Let go of the past, there are bigger and better things to come. You have done well, acted appropriately and now you have the chance to take on more. Legal disputes find in your favour.

Reversed: You don't want to face the truth that the situation has changed. Your fear of the tectonic changes in your life may result in you manufacturing delays, subconsciously or otherwise. But you can not avoid responsibility, and it would be foolish to deny the new opportunities that present themselves. Legal proceedings will find against you. <u>**Do not let fear stop you from seeking help (especially in medical matters).**</u>

The World

ORACLE: YES

KEY WORD GUIDE:

Upright: Success, completion. A sense of unity with the world, or the people around you.
The people who know what you've been through to achieve your goal will congratulate you for your success. But once a goal has been achieved it is time to start on the next part of the journey. Perhaps it is time to travel, broaden your horizons, or take a vacation?
In love: you will find a fulfilling and rewarding relationship.

Reversed: A previous goal has either lost its charm, or you are afraid of successfully achieving it. You might want to back off, but instead you need to act quickly to make the most of the situation before the opportunity passes you by.
You shouldn't envy others their success, if you would put in the same amount of effort yourself, you could achieve similar rewards.

Afterword

I do hope that you find this book helpful in your work with the Tarot and that it proves to be a useful addition to your Tarot collection.

When writing this book I set out to fill in some of the gaps that I found when I first started searching for information on the Tarot. And certainly putting it all down in writing has helped me to focus on the areas that I feel people may want the most guidance with.

I trust that this book answers some of your questions and stimulates you to want to find out more about the Tarot Cards and divination in general. I especially hope that it inspires you to open your channels of communication with your Higher Self, and thus become more in touch with the life force which fills and guides us all through the universal constant of timeless and unconditional love.

In light,
        Eleanor

CPSIA information can be obtained
at www.ICGtesting.com
Printed in the USA
BVHW040052200919
558795BV00007BB/191/P

9 780993 160028